Contents

A Love Connection to God

If you really want to feel close to God
in all that you do every day,
if you want to give God all your love,
what you have to do is pray.

Prayer is your love connection,
and it is really quite easy to do.
For Jesus is patiently waiting
for a love connection with you.

If you are sad and feeling down
about worries or sorrows or cares,
make a love connection;
say God's name,
and ask for help in your prayers.

4

The ABC's of Prayer

...for children

Written by Francine M. O'Connor

Illustrated by Kathryn Boswell

Catechetical Advisers:
The Redemptorists

LIGUORI
PUBLICATIONS

One Liguori Drive
Liguori, Missouri 63057-9999
(314) 464-2500

Imprimi Potest:
William A. Nugent, C.SS.R.
Provincial, St. Louis Province
The Redemptorists

Imprimatur:
Monsignor Maurice F. Byrne
Vice Chancellor, Archdiocese of St. Louis

ISBN 0-89243-317-5
Copyright © 1989, Liguori Publications
Printed in U.S.A.

If happiness is filling your heart,
and you want to sing a song to the Lord,
make a love connection; pray out your joy,
and add a little smile to every word.

If the sun is shining and the breeze is cool,
and the day feels just perfectly grand,
make a love connection; say thanks to God,
who created it all with a loving hand.

You can pray the words you read in this book
or you can pray with words all your own.
You can pray a silent listening prayer
whenever you and God are alone.

Anything at all that connects you with God,
through love or through joy or through tears,
all those things that remind you of God
are your love connections — your prayers.

Prayer Is Listening Too

Prayer is like a long-distance call,
person-to-person between God and you.
It's for thanking, loving, and sharing all;
and prayer is *listening* too.

When you kneel beside your bed at night,
and the words of your prayer won't come,
be quiet and feel the God within you,
warming your heart like the summer sun.

Jesus is always right at your side
whenever you kneel down for prayer.
And the thoughts and sounds that fill you then
are messages of love God wants to share.

Hear God's joy in the whippoorwill's song
or the chirping of crickets after dark.
Feel God's presence in the gentle breeze
that rustles leaves on trees in the park.

Be quiet and know that your God is near,
always ready with great love to share.
And all that you see and hear and feel
are God's wordless answers to your prayer.

Praying With Jesus

Have you ever stopped to wonder
if God really hears you when you pray?
Does it sometimes seem to you as though
the kingdom of heaven is too far away?

Does it make you feel you're all alone
to think that Jesus has gone far away?
Do you wish that he'd come back again
and say, "I'm in your world to stay"?

Jesus knows how you feel.

You see, he was once a child like you,
far from his heavenly home.
When he wanted to stop and talk with God,
he'd go off someplace and pray all alone.

That's why Jesus made this promise:
"Whenever you come together to pray,
I will be there in your midst,
I will hear every prayer that you say."

Now Jesus didn't say he'd be listening
from someplace that's far, far away.
He said he'd come into your very own home
when you and others kneel to pray.

Isn't this a most wonderful thing,
to know that Jesus is always there?
He hears your worries and your fears
and listens to your every prayer.

So don't you wonder, don't you fret.
God *does* hear the words that you pray.
And if God's own Son is praying with you,
can the kingdom of heaven be far away?

Jesus, Teach Me to Pray

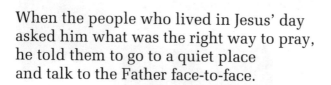

When the people who lived in Jesus' day
asked him what was the right way to pray,
he told them to go to a quiet place
and talk to the Father face-to-face.

He said not to use many words to pray,
for God always knows what you want to say.
Just promise to love God in all that you do,
and ask him, please, to watch over you.

Here is the prayer Jesus taught that day
in words that will help you when you pray.

Heavenly God, your holy name I say.
Help me to do your will today.
All my daily needs will come from you,
for who knows them better than you do?
Please forgive me for the bad things I do,
and I will forgive those who hurt me too.
In temptation, Lord, always make me strong
and, save me from all who would do me wrong.

THE LORD'S PRAYER

Our Father, who art in heaven, hallowed be thy name;
thy kingdom come, thy will be done,
on earth as it is in heaven.
Give us this day our daily bread;
and forgive us our trespasses
as we forgive those who trespass against us;
and lead us not into temptation,
but deliver us from evil.
Amen.

11

My Morning Prayer

I love the look of morning
when early sunlight shines into my room.
I open my eyes to a brand-new day
and forget all about my nighttime gloom.

I love the smells of morning —
the breeze from my window is fresh and fair;
the new-cut grass smells wet with dew
while yummy kitchen odors mingle in the air.

I love the sounds of morning.
Happy voices call out to me.
Dishes rattle, and bacon sizzles
to remind me I'm as hungry as can be!

Good morning, Jesus, my best friend,
I want to thank you once again
for morning things that come my way
to start me on another day.

Thank you for the morning breeze
that wakens me with gentle ease.
Thank you for breakfast to make me strong.
Thank you for blessings this whole day long.

I offer this bright new day to you.
Help me to serve you in all I do.
Keep me safe as I work and play
and once in a while remind me to pray.
Amen.

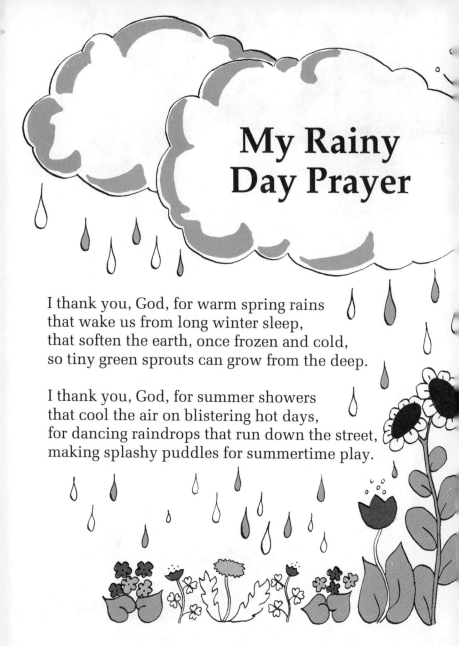

My Rainy Day Prayer

I thank you, God, for warm spring rains
that wake us from long winter sleep,
that soften the earth, once frozen and cold,
so tiny green sprouts can grow from the deep.

I thank you, God, for summer showers
that cool the air on blistering hot days,
for dancing raindrops that run down the street,
making splashy puddles for summertime play.

14

I thank you, God, for the gentle autumn mist
that drips like diamonds off leaves of gold and red.
Once crackly and dry, the leaves will soon become
a soft brilliant blanket for nature's winter bed.

I thank you, God, for winter's freezing rains
that create a crystal fairyland outside.
I thank you for hot cocoa, for indoor family games,
for a cozy fire, and loved ones by my side.

When I hear the pitter-patter, drip, drop, splash
or watch the trickling streams on my windowpane,
when new flowers grow or cool breezes blow,
I thank you, God, for your precious gift of rain.
Amen.

A Valentine Prayer

Dear Jesus, on this Valentine's Day
will you be my valentine?
Will you take your special love,
and set it in this heart of mine?

When I am feeling alone and small
like a tiny ship in a mighty sea,
remind me of your loving call,
"Let the children come to me."

When I fight with my good friend,
as even best friends sometimes do,
let your commandment be my light,
"Love one another as I love you."

When I see someone hungry and poor,
remind me about the good I can do.
"Do to others," says your golden rule,
"as you would have them do to you."

When people are lonely or sick or sad,
and I am too busy to help or to see,
may I remember the words you said,
"What you do for them, you do for me."

Help me, Jesus, to be like you —
gentle and thoughtful and kind.
Then I will be your valentine,
just as you will always be mine.
Amen.

Mary, Mary, Lovely Lady

Mary, Mary, lovely lady,
why did God choose you to be
the Mother of his Son on earth
and a special example for me?

Were you always the very best one
at home or at play or at school?
Did you always behave just as you should
and obey each commandment and rule?

Did you remember God all of the time,
even when you were out playing ball?
Or when the lake was just right for a swim,
did you stop and thank God for it all?

Did you help your parents without being asked
and pick up your toys when playtime was done?
Did you always get along with all of your friends
and never get angry or fight with just one?

Did you always sit still when you were in church
and never giggle or wiggle about?
Did you close your eyes to say your prayers
and say them softly and not shout them out?

Well, that's how I try to be most of the time,
but I don't always turn out so good.
Then I think about you, who were chosen by God,
and pray to act more as a Christian should.

Now, Mary, Mary, lovely lady,
I'm so happy that God chose you,
for it helps me remember, most of the time,
that God has chosen me too!
Amen.

My Thanksgiving Prayer

Bartimaeus, the blind man, sat by the road
in a world without beauty or light.
Then Jesus touched his unseeing eyes
and gave him the great gift of sight.
Lord, thank you for letting me see this day.

A sick man lay by the side of a pool
where suffering people were made right.
Jesus said, "Walk!" and the happy man danced
while the people looked on in delight.
Lord, thank you for the chance to run and play.

Some people brought a sick friend to Jesus,
but the crowd wouldn't let them come in.
So down through the roof they lowered his bed
to the place where Jesus waited for him.
Lord, thank you for those who bring me to you.

The apostles and Jesus were out in a boat
when a terrible storm came along.
"Jesus, save us!" they cried out loud.
Jesus waved his hand, and the storm was gone.
Lord, thank you for calming my fears.

When Jesus' good friend Lazarus died,
Jesus felt great sorrow and pain.
He went to the tomb and called him by name,
and the friend who was dead lived again!
Lord, thank you for heaven and life without end.

When Jesus was teaching down by the shore,
the children all gathered at his knee.
When grownups tried to send them away,
Jesus said, "Let the children come to me."
Thank you, Jesus, for being my friend.
Amen!

My "Yes" to God

When other kids are being bad,
when ugly words are being said,
when things are done that make God sad,
I'll say no to that!

When temptation starts to get too strong,
when things look right but are really wrong,
when someone says, "Just go along!"
I'll say no to that!

I believe in God the Father,
creator of our world so wide.
I believe in Jesus Christ,
who for me was crucified.
I believe in the Holy Spirit,
sent by God to be my guide.
I say yes to that!

I believe in the Catholic Church
and all the saints in heaven too.
I know that God forgives my sins
and helps me to begin anew.
I say yes to that!

Father, Son, and Holy Spirit,
help me keep each promise true.
Make me strong and wise and good
so I can always follow you.
Amen.

Happiness Prayer

Thank you, dear God, for happy things —
for buzzing bees and butterfly wings,
for budding trees in the early spring,
for flying high on the playground swing.

Thank you, dear God, for this happy day,
for those who love me in every way,
for the soft, warm touch of a summer ray,
for my best friend and the games we play.
Amen.

Prayer Before Mass

I kneel before your altar, Lord,
and pray to understand your Word,
to not let silly thoughts disturb
the prayer-thoughts my heart has heard.

I'll smile at the people when I pass
I'll stand or kneel as the grownups do.
I'll close my eyes and say a prayer
and think about your love so true.
Amen.

Prayer for My Family

You knew me, God, when I was small,
before I could speak a word at all.
I couldn't play jacks or catch a ball
or even walk without a fall.

Then you gave your first gift to me,
the loving members of my family.
They added my name to our family tree
and taught me to be the best I can be.

Now I thank you, God, for this special grace
and for each loving smile and gentle face.
For granting me a special place
in my family of love for all my days.
Amen.

Communion Prayer

Jesus in the Communion bread,
I know that you are really here.
I've come especially because
I always love to have you near.

When we receive you in our hearts,
We feel your presence ever dear.
Jesus in the Communion bread,
come to us as we kneel here.
Amen.

I'm Sorry, Lord

Jesus, you know so much about me,
you know when I'm happy and when I'm sad.
You know that I try very hard to be good,
and you know I'm sorry when I'm bad.

Forgive me now for all those times
when I have failed to follow you.
You're the best friend I've ever had,
my God, my brother, and teacher too.
Amen.

Prayer to the Holy Spirit

Holy Spirit sent by God,
be my guide along the way.
Teach me all I need to know
to follow Jesus every day.

Gentle as a summer breeze,
hushed as a whisper in my ear,
quietly you live within me,
stilling every doubt and fear.

Let my mind grow in your wisdom,
let my heart grow in your love.
Stay with me, and I shall be
truly blessed by God above.
Amen.

My Bedtime Prayer

Thank you, God, for happy things,
like spending time with people I love,
like silly rhymes with made-up lines,
and birdsongs and breezes
and sunshine above.

And thank you, Lord,
for showing me things,
like the fish that swim
in the brook,
like walks in the woods
when leaves turn bright,
and reading the stories
in my favorite book.

And thank you, God,
for loving things,
like spicy-kitchen smells
on Thanksgiving day,
like Mommy's arms
when things go wrong,
like a phone call
from those
who live far away.

Please help the families all over the world,
especially those who are poor or sad.
Help them know how much you love them today
so they will know the same joy that I have had.

Lord, you take care of my family
every minute throughout the year.
I'm glad you give me this time to pray
and thank you for your loving care.

And thank you, God, for quiet things,
like snowflakes that silently fall in the night,
like good-night kisses that brush my face
when loved ones come to tuck me in tight.
Amen.

31

MORE CHILDREN'S BOOKS

by Francine M. O'Connor

The ABC's of the Old Testament...for children

Children will enjoy this collection of twelve stories from the Old Testament. Lively verse and colorful illustrations help little ones understand that the God who cared for the people of the Old Testament is the same God who watches over and loves them today. **$2.95**

The ABC's of the Sacraments...for children

Introduces children to both familiar and yet-to-be-introduced sacraments. It touches on each of these important elements of faith with verses and illustrations that celebrate God's loving presence at these special moments. A delightful way to help young children understand Baptism, Eucharist, Confirmation, Matrimony, and the other sacraments. **$2.95**

The ABC's of the Mass...for children

This creative combination of verse and illustration moves step by step through the various parts of the Mass and includes explanations of some of the prayers that children hear in every liturgy — but often don't fully understand. **$2.95**

The ABC's of the Rosary...for children

This little book does more than merely teach the formula and the prayers — it highlights each of the fifteen mysteries in a fascinating presentation that brings the story of Jesus and his mother to life. This book makes the rosary a prayer experience the whole family can share. **$2.95**

Order from your local bookstore or write to
Liguori Publications
Box 060, Liguori, Missouri 63057-9999
For faster service, call toll-free (800) 325-9521, ext. 060.,
8 a.m. to 4 p.m. Central time
*(Please add $1.00 for postage and handling
for orders under $5.00; $1.50 for orders over $5.00.)*